SUICIDAL CHILDREN AND ADOLESCENTS

Crisis and Preventive Care

Sheila Rioch

ISBN   0 9523281 0 0

Published by Celia Publications, Durham.
First published in 1994

First re-print   :   August 1994
Second re-print :   March 1995

Other titles by the same author :

'Job Loss and Unemployment - The Manager's Role'
'The Leader's Role During Change'

Designed and printed by Jamel Graphics Limited, Durham.

CONTENTS

SECTION THREE - PREVENTION AND QUALITY CARE AUDIT

LIST OF TABLES

ACKNOWLEDGEMENTS

I would like to thank colleagues in the United Kingdom and overseas who over the years have demonstrated how to provide innovative and high quality care to sad and desolate children and adolescents entrusted to their care.

I should also like to thank Matthew for illustrating the book.

PREFACE

Suicide destroys a high number of our young people in the prime of their lives. This book attempts to address a social and health problem that is affecting all sections of society, both nationally and internationally, the problem of suicidal children and adolescents.

As we approach the twenty-first century suicide is now the second most common cause of death in young people in the United Kingdom, United States of America and Canada. The tragedy of this rising number of suicidal children and adolescents is a cause of concern to both families and carers. This book has been written in an attempt to raise awareness throughout society of the extent of the problem.

The author assumes that society places a high value on life and would, therefore, wish to play a part in a collective endeavour to reduce the number of suicidal children and adolescents. Although the title and contents of this book may appear pessimistic, the intention is to provide indicators for action that could lead to a more optimistic future for young people.

The author is aware that in-depth study of a subject can blind one to the existence of wider perspectives and alternative lines of enquiry as the subject is studied in more depth. It is hoped that these limiting factors will stimulate further debate, research and action into the tragic subject of suicidal children and adolescents. As we progress through the nineteen-nineties towards the twenty-first century we can all play a part in an endeavour to reduce those appalling statistics in order to enable our young people to look with hope to their future.

GLOSSARY

Assessment   -   A process of evaluating a person's condition, in an individual or group setting, with a view to determining how the condition should be dealt with[1].

Attempted Suicide   -   The non-fatal act of self-injury undertaken with conscious self-destructive intent, however vague and unambiguous[2]

Child   -   Children and adolescents i.e., young people.

Parent   -   Biological or substitute parent.

Professional Carer   -   A person employed to work in a crisis situation with the suicidal child, parents and family.

Society   -   The human race, worldwide.

Stigma   -   A slur attached to a person's reputation.

Suicide   -   The fatal outcome of a suicide act.

Taboo   -   Unmentionable.

INTRODUCTION

It has been acknowledged that the attempted suicide and suicide rates of young people are rising in Western Europe, Northern America and beyond [1], and it would appear that this suicidal behaviour has no boundaries and no guarantee of immunity as the rates continue to rise.

Perhaps we need to ask ourselves why is it that some young people wish to die rather than to live, especially at a time when great progress is being made in scientific and technological research and development. Why is it that good psychological and mental health would appear to be less highly thought of than good physical health? Could it be connected in any way with our achievement-oriented society? Perhaps it is that search for constant happiness, a society where there is no pain? Regrettably life is not like that and therefore we need to enable our young children and adolescents to find ways of managing the emotional traumas and difficulties that may come their way. They also require help to recognise when psychological and mental health care may be needed, either personally or for their friends and peers.

Suicidal behaviour is a complex subject and there would appear to be no simple explanation for the cause of the behaviour [2, 3, 4, 5]. When a young person dies following a suicidal act, a parent may be made to feel that he, or she, has been a bad parent, although Wrobleski has identified that there are 'good' parents whose children commit suicide and 'bad' parents whose children do not commit suicide [6].

Governments and agencies, internationally, are slowly becoming aware that :

- more needs to be done to raise the profile of children and adolescents, and

- ways to improve the emotional well-being of children and adolescents need to be found [7, 8].

However, these declarations of intent have come at a time of competing market forces, within government departments and agencies, for the limited financial resources that are available.

In this book an attempt will be made to answer some of the questions concerning suicidal behaviour, especially the question:

'What can we do, as carers and members of society, to help reduce the incidents of suicidal behaviour in young people?'

It is unlikely that there will ever be sufficient health workers, clergy, social workers and voluntary workers to care for those young people who are desolate, depressed and in despair. Members of society will also be needed and should be encouraged to join forces with the professionals in an endeavour to reverse the increase of suicidal behaviour in young people [5, 9].

In the first section of this book a selection of literature on suicide is explored and includes statistical and general information on suicidal behaviour. Details of causes, precipitating factors and methods used by suicidal young people are covered in the second chapter. In section two the care of the suicidal young person, the importance of family-centred care and how this may ultimately be of benefit to the young person who attempts suicide is explored.

An account of the interpersonal and practical care that may be required by the family following the suicide of a young person is provided in chapter five.

In section three the topic of preventive care is investigated; this is followed by conclusions and recommendations that could have some impact on the endeavour to reduce the number of suicidal young people.

An audit tool, in the form of a check list, is included in Appendix A to enable carers to evaluate either their own performance, or the performance of their staff.

A list of names and addresses of organisations that are able to :

- provide help and advice for the suicidal young person and the family, and

- provide support for the parents and family following suicide of a young person

can be found in Appendix B.

SECTION ONE

GENERAL INFORMATION

LITERATURE REVIEW

In this chapter literature on suicide and relevant issues is explored and includes statistical information, attitudes of society towards suicide, international reports and research studies on child care. The chapter concludes with a brief reference to the emotional development of the child.

STATISTICAL INFORMATION

The problem of the rising rate of suicides in young people may appear insignificant in some countries when compared with other countries [1] (Table I). However, for the parent with a child who dies as a result of a suicidal act, a statistic is of little significance in relation to the emotional anguish experienced following the child's death. A comprehensive analysis of European suicide statistics was compiled in the nineteenth century and demonstrated a difference in suicide rates between cultures [2]. A high ratio of male to female suicides was identified on that occasion and is still present today (Tables 1, 2 and 3).

The reliability of those statistics is regarded with scepticism and an underestimation of deaths from suicide in young people is widely reported [2,3,4,5]. The rise in suicide statistics, although understated, appears to imply that there is an increase in the number of sad, desolate and depressed children and adolescents within society today.

On endeavouring to obtain statistics on suicide attempts of young people it becomes apparent that there is not a formal system of record keeping. In the majority of countries there is no requirement for these statistics to be collected and recorded [5,6,7]. Estimates on the ratio of suicide attempts to suicide among the population of young people vary across a wide range from:

- 100 attempts : 1 suicide [6]
    to
- 312 attempts : 1 suicide [7].

The figure of 312 attempts to 1 suicide is based on a specific study of fifteen to eighteen year old young people, other figures stated in studies appear to be estimates [7]. It has been found that the young person who attempts suicide may make another attempt although a problem then arises of not knowing

TABLE 1 - SELECTION OF COUNTRIES - MALE SUICIDES

YEAR	COUNTRY	NUMBER OF DEATHS	
		5-14 YEARS	15-24 YEARS
1991	Iceland	-	13 (61.0)
1991	Finland	3 (0.9)	139 (42.2)
1989	New Zealand	8 (3.1)	111 (37.9)
1990	Canada	23 (1.2)	484 (24.6)
1989	United States	184 (1.0)	4106 (22.2)
1990	Norway	4 (1.5)	74 (22.1)
1990	Sweden	-	120 (19.8)
1991	Hungary	7 (1.0)	154 (19.6)
1990	Poland	39 (1.2)	441 (15.8)
1990	Ireland	4 (1.2)	44 (14.2)
1990	France	14 (0.4)	607 (14.1)
1991	United Kingdom	4 (0.1)	481 (11.5)

World Health Organisation (1993)

(Figure in brackets is the age-specific rate per 100,000 population.)

TABLE 2.   SELECTION OF COUNTRIES - FEMALE SUICIDES

		NUMBER OF DEATHS	
YEAR	COUNTRY	5-14 YEARS	15-24 YEARS
1990	Sweden	2 (0.4)	48 (8.3)
1991	Finland	-	23 (7.3)
1989	New Zealand	-	20 (7.0)
1990	Norway	-	20 (6.3)
1991	Hungary	2 (0.3)	40 (5.3)
1990	Canada	7 (0.4)	94 (5.0)
1991	Iceland	1 (4.9)	1 (4.9)
1990	France	5 (0.1)	184 (4.4)
1989	United States	56 (0.3)	764 (4.2)
1990	Ireland	-	12 (4.1)
1990	Poland	8 (0.2)	64 (2.4)
1991	United Kingdom	1	93 (2.3)

World Heath Organisation (1993)

(Figure in brackets is the age-specific rate per 100,000 population.)

TABLE 3. SELECTION OF EUROPEAN COUNTRIES - 1874-1878
RATE OF SUICIDES PER MILLION INHABITANTS

COUNTRY	SUICIDE RATE
Denmark	255
France	160
Sweden	91
Norway	71
England	69
Italy	38

Modified Durkheim.

precisely who will make a further attempt [3, 8]. The critical period for another suicide attempt would appear to be during the four years following the first attempt [3], and with 10 - 14% of young people making a further attempt within twelve months [5].

As suicide is now the second leading cause of death in young people in the United Kingdom, Canada, The United States and beyond it can no longer be considered the rare occurrence as reported by Durkheim in the nineteenth century [2].

ATTITUDES TO SUICIDE

Suicide is almost as old as man and although attitudes of society concerning suicide are considered to be more enlightened now, when compared to earlier periods, there is still a stigma attached to the suicide act in many cultures [9, 10, 11]. Doubt has also been expressed whether the majority of the population accepts suicide [12]. Opinion has changed over the centuries from apparent acceptance and approval of suicide to the present disapproval. At one time suicide was accepted as reasonable when it was chosen to :

- save another's life

- avoid a great evil

- defend the country

- prove devotion.

In the third century A.D. the Bishop of Caesarea was reported to have advised his Christian followers to embrace suicide as a form of protest against the government of the time [6]. Curran indicated that attitudes towards suicide changed radically in the fourth century A.D. when rules were laid down against suicide by St Augustine [7].

At present there are world religions that oppose suicide and therefore the family would not wish information to be disclosed should suicide take place [3, 4]. Although no longer a criminal offence in many countries, it remains a criminal offence to assist a person in the act of suicide in some countries.

Professional carers, on occasions, may display prejudice towards both the child who attempts suicide and the family of the child who dies following a suicidal act [6, 9, 10]. Carers are advised to be aware of their prejudices when caring for the young person and family. Consciously or unconsciously the child becomes aware of adult prejudices and may be unwilling to admit to feeling unhappy or depressed since this could be interpreted as a sign of weakness [12, 13]. Curran indicated that the adolescent desires to feel independent and able to take control of his or her problems, and that to be incapacitated in any way is anathema to the teenager [7].

MEANING AND VALUE OF LIFE

Questions on the meaning and value of life, and the threat to an individual's liberty need consideration when the topic of suicide is discussed [14, 15]. When a child is involved, and is under the legal age of consent, additional questions have to be asked. Should the young person be allowed to take his or her own life if that is desired? If that young person is so emotionally wounded, and would prefer to die, should one intervene? Philosophers appear to agree that when a person is psychologically impaired the carer should intervene [14, 15]. However, it was stated from a different source that a person "is free to decide to take his, or her, own life if he, or she, chooses, no matter what their age" [16]. This statement appears to conflict with recent guidelines which state that :
"The age and competence of the child should be taken into account when deciding what degree of intervention is necessary" [17].

STUDIES AND REPORTS ON SUICIDAL BEHAVIOUR

The studies and reports indicate that children and adolescents who attempt suicide should be admitted to the local accident and emergency department for care; and that follow-up care should be family centred [5, 6, 18]. However, it was acknowledged that the family may be a factor that had contributed to the child's suicide attempt, therefore an initial assessment with the young person, alone, by a member of the Child and Adolescent Mental Health Care Team was advised [19].

It was indicated that :

- approximately one-third of the young people could be transferred to community follow-up care and treatment from the general practitioner

- a minority of young people may require residential care, and

- on occasions the young person may become so disturbed that secure accommodation is necessary [5, 20].

The prognosis following a suicide attempt appears to be uncertain and the low attendance rate at some Child and Adolescent Mental Health Clinics for follow-up care is a cause of concern [5].

It was advised that a strategy for suicide prevention among young people should be introduced without delay, although it was acknowledged that it is not possible to identify the most effective prevention programme of those currently in use [8, 9]. It was recommended that small-scale local programmes on suicide prevention should be implemented and evaluated [8].

The detrimental effect of financial poverty on the psychological and mental health of the family and child has been well-documented [21, 22, 23]. Hewlett identified an additional cause of poverty in two affluent countries; the scarcity of parental time. It was implied that parents are failing to invest time in the raising of their children who are being left to cope with the difficult business of growing up in the 1990's [24].

An increase in depressive illness among adolescents and young adults was identified by Klerman who indicated that the age of onset of depression was now lower than in earlier decades [25]. An increase in alcohol and drug dependency among young people was also reported as being a possible contributory factor to the rise in suicide and attempted suicides. Bradshaw implied that alcohol and drugs could bring about dramatic mood changes when taken by young people [26].

The actual cause of suicidal behaviour is now known to be multi-factorial, involving an interplay of genetic and environmental factors. Recent work by Fahy in Ireland, and American researchers has identified that severe depressive illness can result when a chemical substance in the brain, serotonin, is depleted [8, 27]. The importance of early detection of depression in young people, as part of a suicide prevention programme was recommended [5, 28].

EMOTIONAL DEVELOPMENT OF THE CHILD

In the final paragraph of this chapter the emotional development of the child is briefly discussed. The work of Bowlby has influenced the study of young children and their development for several decades [29, 30]. The Bowlby theory on attachment is concerned with the early separation of a young child from the parent, and the detrimental effect on the developing child following the separation. Bradshaw indicated that young children are resilient and have an innate optimism and trust in people since they believe that the world is a friendly place. However, children are vulnerable and that trust and optimism can become blunted through misunderstanding or violation from a parent [26]. Recent work has highlighted problems that can arise between a parent and child, through communication difficulties, when the child receives the wrong message. The child may develop common behavioural problems that include:

- temper tantrums

- separation fears, and

- sleeping difficulties [31].

The increasing number of working women who need to have a reliable parent substitute to care for their young child is not always supported by Governments. Siegart and Leach report that up-dating of old-fashioned employment practice has not taken place in all countries [32]. Finally, it has recently been stated that in the Anglo-American world : "Parents are devoting much more time to earning a living and much less time to their children than they did a generation ago" [24]. The growing economic pressures on families with children could indicate that the parent(s) will need to be a part of the labour force for the foreseeable future..

Finally, there are historical accounts of the unhappy and desolate child, and of the young people, who lived in large institutions and foundling hospitals during the eighteenth, nineteenth and twentieth centuries. In the majority of countries those large institutions are no longer in existence; however, the problems of the unhappy and desolate child is still present.

2.   SUICIDE RISK FACTORS

The reason that a young person decides to end his or her life is complex and still not fully understood, and in many cases a cause is not identified following the death [1, 2, 3]. Stengel indicated that suicide is a gamble with life that may or may not come off [3].

CAUSES

Recent studies indicate that the causes of suicide are multiple and that it is a combination of factors that influence the behaviour of the young person [4, 5, 6, 7]. The following factors were identified :

- biological
- genetic
- psychological
- social, and
- impulse

Durkheim, a century ago, implied that although suicide attempts may be treated medically as an individual phenomenon, the cause could lie deep in the social life-history of the young person [8]. Recent studies emphasise the interplay between genetic and environmental factors, also the onset of depression at a lower age along with an increase in the use of drugs and alcohol appear to influence suicide risk [9].

The underlying cause of suicidal behaviour may at first be overlooked as the precipitating factor assumes prominence. This factor may have caused the scales to tip in favour of the young person making a decision to die rather than to live [3]. The mystery remains, however, as not all children affected by the aforementioned factors will attempt suicide. Many emotionally deprived young people do not attempt suicide and many young people who have an apparently affluent and comfortable childhood do commit suicide [2, 10].

Additional underlying factors that may influence the behaviour of young people include :

- the increasing demands of a competitive society and the high expectations of parents for their children which may cause unacceptable levels of stress, and

- urban living, especially in inner city areas.

Recent research into the effect of inner city life identified the unhappiness experienced by adolescents who declared that life was not worth living for 15% of those young people [11].

PRECIPITATING FACTORS

The precipitating factors that may lead to a suicide attempt and suicide include :

- physical abuse

- sexual abuse

- a row with parents, boyfriend or girlfriend

- a loss of a parent caused by death, separation or divorce

- unwanted pregnancy

- under investigation by the police

- in police custody (on remand)

- unemployment

- rape

- bullying

- poor examination results.

The following two factors, which overlap the two categories of precipitating factors and warning signs and symptoms, and cause great concern to carers and parents are :

- substance abuse which includes drugs, alcohol and solvents, and

- the eating disorders of anorexia and bulimia.

WARNING SIGNS AND SYMPTOMS

Warning signs and symptoms that may alert carers, family and friends to the possibility that the young person could be at risk of suicide are numerous and include :

- a decline in school performance

- anti-social behaviour, for example truancy and shoplifting

- low self-esteem

- relationship difficulties with parents

- social isolation

- stress, anxiety and despair

- clash of cultures

- loss of appetite and withdrawn

- chronic ill-health and refusal to take medications

- self harm.

10, 12, 13

Crook reported that on occasions a young person may give away his or her clothes, books, video and tapes, prior to the suicide act.

Warning signs and symptoms may include mood changes and an exhibition of violent behaviour; the young person may also demonstrate :

- either an attitude of hopelessness and despair

- or rebellion which may result in running away from home and becoming a homeless person.

When a child or adolescent threatens suicide, or makes remarks that are suggestive of suicide, it is recommended that these warnings are taken seriously and not lightly dismissed. [2, 3, 10]

Many of the aforementioned precipitating factors, warning signs and symptoms may be identified before a suicide attempt is made. The difficulty lies in predicting which young person will carry out a suicide act. When action is not taken to prevent a suicide attempt, or if that action is unsuccessful, then one of the following methods may be used by the young person in an endeavour to end his or her life.

METHODS

The method used for the suicide act can be classified as violent or non-violent and is likely to depend on what is available to the young person [3, 14]. The classification of violent and non-violent could be questioned by carers who may consider that all the stated methods appear to be violent (table 4).

TABLE 4

SUICIDAL ACT - METHOD USED

Violent	Non-Violent	
Jump from a height	Tablets	) with/without
Hanging	Drug injection	) alcohol
Lying on a railway line	Plastic bag(s) over head and face	
Gun shot to self	Inhalation of car exhaust fumes	
Slashed wrists/throat	Drowning	
Set fire to self		

A manual published recently in Japan includes freezing oneself, and driving into quicksands as additional methods used for the suicide act.

The place where a young person attempts suicide could be the deciding factor on whether the person lives or dies [3]. He or she may be discovered accidentally, and live, or tragically may die in a room when other family members are in the same house [15]. Occasionally a young person may be missing for days and eventually the body may be found some distance from the family home [16].

The fact revealed in suicide studies is that many young people appear reluctant to seek help when they are experiencing despair, isolation or depression. In the next chapter the care of the young person after a suicide attempt will be explored.

SECTION TWO

INTERPERSONAL AND PRACTICAL CARE

3. ATTEMPTED SUICIDE

It was stated by Stengel that life will never be the same again for a young person who attempts suicide [1]. Whether the child or adolescent is admitted to hospital or not the young person has indirectly acknowledged that help is required, he or she has made an appeal for help.

Health carers appear to agree that young people who attempt suicide should be admitted to hospital for a social and mental health assessment by a member of the child and adolescent mental health care team [2, 3, 4].

POWER OF THE PROFESSIONAL

Many young people, following a suicide attempt, are taken to their local accident and emergency hospital department for immediate physical care. The child and parent, who at the time of the crisis are in a vulnerable position, may feel threatened by the power that the health carers appear to have over them. The attitude and manner of the carer can have a profound effect on the young person and parent and may influence whether the care offered is accepted or rejected.

Health carers, occasionally, appear to be unaware that all suicide attempts are serious and that a sad, desolate and possibly depressed young person is depending on them to provide care in a non-judgmental way.. Young people are sensitive and may be embarrassed about their privacy, and their body, and could strongly object at having soiled clothing removed by a stranger following admission to hospital [5]. Fear and anxiety can also result in violent and abusive reaction from a young person, especially in response to any necessary physical treatment [6]. It was observed by Crook that some nurses and doctors did not appear to understand the problems experienced by suicidal children and adolescents, and were judgmental and critical towards them. It was advised that an adult should remain with the young person in the accident and emergency department in order to provide support and to act as an advocate on his or her behalf [4].

INTERPERSONAL CARE

An assessment on the possibility of a further suicide attempt will need to be performed by a health carer when the person is admitted to the accident and emergency department [6]. Great patience may be required from the health carer, to enable the young person to talk and disclose the extent of his or her sorrow and despair, as difficulty may be experienced when discussing personal emotions [7]. A parent may be unable to wait with the child indefinitely in the department especially if a younger child has been left unattended at home, or with a neighbour; however, it is essential that the young person is not left alone if the parent has to leave as another suicide attempt may be made, and could be fatal.

Much publicity has recently been given to the lengthy period that patients spend waiting in accident and emergency departments until a bed becomes available in the hospital ward. This could be regarded as unacceptable high-risk practice should a suicidal young person be detained in the department for a lengthy period, or alternatively, when a bed is made available in an inappropriate ward in the hospital. After admission to either the child and adolescent ward, or medical ward in the case of the mature adolescent who may be more than sixteen years, the young person's emotional and mental state should be assessed by a member of the Child and Adolescent Mental Health Care Team. The waiting period for this assessment should not exceed twenty-four hours although this period is likely to vary from under twelve hours to more than seventy two hours, depending on the resources available at the local hospital. During this waiting period the health carer will be required to provide the necessary care to help reduce the young person's emotional pain.

THE VULNERABLE YOUNG PERSON

Throughout the period that the young person remains in hospital the health carers have a valuable role to play and should, therefore, have the necessary skills to care for the child or adolescent during this period of vulnerability. If the young person has to wait several days before an assessment of psychological and mental health is undertaken then, during that waiting period, other health carers will be required to provide appropriate care in an endeavour to help reduce the young person's distress and despair. Appropriate care should include :

- giving full attention to the child or adolescent

- providing an atmosphere that is free from distraction and that

encourages the child or adolescent to talk
- hearing what is being said by the child or adolescent
- demonstrating a gentle and caring manner that enables the young person to express feelings
- demonstrating patience and encouragement towards the young person.

Information should be made available in writing on the names and addresses of agencies where help can be obtained, should the young person feel unable to confide in a family member. It is unlikely that the person will remember verbal information that is given during this period of emotional crisis.

AFTER CARE

Non judgmental care, referred to in a preceding paragraph, will also be required when the young person returns to his, or her, social environment. Confidentiality of information concerning the child or adolescent is important, although other carers within the community who are able to provide :
- supportive care and encouragement, and
- help to enable the young person rebuild his or her self-esteem

may need to be aware of the crisis.

Crook identified parents as the most important people in the life of a teenager in a study undertaken into attempted suicide of teenagers [4]. It was also found that parents needed much more help in order to identify signs and symptoms of suicidal behaviour in young people. The teenagers identified that :
- they needed discreet care, as they valued their independence and
- they wanted to be able to talk to their parents [4]

Health carers appear to agree that a few young people may need further intensive care of their mental and emotional state in specialised units; however, the majority of young people return to the community for their emotional care [3, 8].

To conclude this chapter a brief reference will be made on the availability of resources, as it is unlikely that there will ever be enough health carers, social workers, ministers and teachers to identify, and care for the rising number of suicidal young people [1, 9]. Society will, therefore, be required to play a major role in helping to identify those sad, desolate and depressed children and adolescents; and also help to provide a more supportive and caring environment for our young people.

In a later chapter, on preventive care, suggestions are made on the action that can be undertaken with young people in an endeavour to provide support and care.

In the next chapter care of the family following the young person's suicide attempt is discussed.

4.   FOLLOWING A SUICIDE ATTEMPT

A young person who attempts suicide may not have wanted to die, given the chance of a better life, and because he, or she, is still alive there is now time for the family and friends to respond to the young person's cry for help.

REACTION OF THE FAMILY

The reaction of the parents and family members to the suicide is likely to be one of shock or horror. To the professional carer the reaction can appear similar to a grief response, with a display of self-blame, anger, remorse and fear [1]. The effect on the family of attempted suicide by one of its members has been described as complex and varied, with an appeal factor appearing strong at first. However, those feelings could be replaced by anger, at a later stage, if reasons for the suicidal behaviour are not fully understood by the parents and family.

INTERPERSONAL CARE OF THE PARENTS

A quiet room should be made available as the parent will need to be able to voice personal concerns and anxieties in a comfortable non-threatening environment. The parent may appear tense and intimidated by the hospital atmosphere and staff, especially if a lengthy wait had been experienced in the accident and emergency department. There is a possibility that the parent may wish to take the child home following any medical treatment, before a social and mental health assessment has been undertaken. An endeavour should be made to ensure that the parent is aware that the suicide attempt is a cry for help, and that their child could benefit from professional health care as other factors may be causing the distress, in addition to a stated precipitating factor.

The parent may wish to unburden themselves to the health carer and they should be helped to understand :

- how they can work towards raising their child's self-esteem,

- that they still have time to work with the young person, and can receive further help if necessary, and

- that they have an opportunity to demonstrate that they care.

The parents may be concerned that the young person will be removed from the home. Reassurance should be given that if this does become necessary for the safety of the child, then the parents should endeavour not to blame themselves [2].

If previous suicide attempts have been made by the young person then the 'cry for help' message may need to be reinforced.

AFTER-EFFECT OF THE SUICIDE ATTEMPT

After a suicide attempt the young person is usually removed from the family home and taken to the local hospital. This unexpected action may help to reinforce the fact that the young person has experienced a crisis in his or her life. Wright stated that a crisis 'is something which disturbs old habits and evokes the potential for new responses' [1]. The crisis could lead to a change in the relationship between the parents and their child, and may result in either an improvement, or a deterioration, of the relationship.

Stengel implied that punitive reactions towards a young person, following a suicide attempt are rare; although a parent may react with anger and regard the suicide attempt as an act directed against them. Alternatively, there may be an upsurge of tenderness towards the child, as the parent is overcome by guilt and remorse [3].

INFORMATION AND CONTINUING CARE

The parents and the family should be given information, in writing, of the different agencies that can provide assistance should the need arise. Family-centred care may, or may not, be available and will depend on where the family happen to live. Crook implied that some family-centred care is good, and some may not be as good. This depends on the skills and availability of professional carers [4].

Most organisations are able to respond to a crisis situation and it is the follow-up care that may be patchy. A problem may also arise, concerning clinic attendance for follow-up care, as the parents and child may fail to attend the clinic [5].

The Child Psychotherapy Trust is a registered charitable organisation, and operates in England. This organisation was established for the purpose of providing psychological care of children and the family [6]. Favourable reports on recent work provide evidence on the need to extend this type of care.

In the next chapter the practical and interpersonal care of the family, following the suicide of a young person, will be explored. Although carers are advised to examine their own feelings about death, in order to be in a position to provide effective care of the bereaved, [7, 8] it needs to be recognised that many people, including professional carers, are reluctant either to think about their own death or the death of their children.

5.   SUICIDE OF A YOUNG PERSON

Suicide of a child, or adolescent, is one of the greatest tragedies and is likely to have a far reaching effect, especially on parents, other family members and the community. Much publicity is given locally, nationally and occasionally internationally, to the young person who dies following a suicide act; however, the anguish felt by the family does not appear to receive consideration. It is the anguish of the parents and family members that will be examined in this chapter.

CARE OF THE FAMILY

It has been indicated that the professional carer's attitude and manner towards the family, following the discovery of the young person's body, will have a significant effect on how the family members cope in the weeks, months and years ahead [1]. The social stigma that still appears to be attached to suicide could mean that the professional carer, whom the family will meet immediately after the suicide or suspected suicide, may need to suspend their own feelings in order to provide comfort and support, in addition to the practical care, for the parents and other family members. One of the reasons that it is considered helpful to examine one's own feelings, concerning suicide, is to gain an awareness of the strong personal emotions that may be aroused when caring for the family of the dead child.

The person who finds the body could be a parent, brother, sister or stranger and is likely to be deeply shocked at the discovery. Other family members will also experience disbelief or shock when they are informed of the death [2,3]. The immediate reaction of the parents and family to the news will vary and range from hysterical screaming to a numb silence. The parents and family members should be able to shout and scream within a private room, especially if they are being cared for in a busy treatment area. The emotions of the parents are likely to be intense as they become aware that there is no way their child can be helped now that the final act has taken place and the child is dead [4]. The parents are unlikely to be able to find out why their child chose suicide, if this is confirmed; the child is no longer there and is unable to say why death was preferred to life. The family will need much support when being asked to make decisions concerning the young person's body, following the death.

PRACTICAL CONSIDERATIONS

One of the first decisions that the parents may be asked to make could concern the formal identification, and viewing, of the young person's body. There are usually ways of preparing a body, which may be severely mutilated, that can disguise unsightly and disfiguring parts thereby making the procedure less traumatic for the parents. Each member of the family should be allowed to make their own decision on whether to say 'goodbye', or not, to the young person before the body is removed to the undertaker's premises.

Should a parent or family member decide not to see the dead child or adolescent, immediately following the suicide, then they should be made aware that there could be a further opportunity to say 'goodbye' at the undertaker's premises. The parents and family may wish to assist in the preparation of the young person for burial, with the help of the undertaker [5].

It has been indicated that although a parent may regret, at a later date, not taking the opportunity to say 'goodbye' to their child that decision should be made by the parent [6].

The parents should be advised that an inquest will be necessary, and that this procedure is always taken to establish the cause of death, if possible, of an unexpected death. In the absence of a suicide note a verdict of suicide may not be made, as the coroner has to be certain that the young person intended to take his or her own life.

The expense of the funeral may be an unexpressed anxiety for parents and information, in writing, on grants that are available should be given to the parents.

ROLE OF DIFFERENT AGENCIES

There are many different professional carers who may meet the parents and family within a short time of the child's death, and these include :

- Police officers who may have to inform the parents of the death of their child.

- Health carers who may care for the parents at the local hospital.

- Ministers of Religion who may meet the parents to arrange the burial of the child.

- Teachers who may either be present if the death occurs on the school premises, or, may be informed by the parents of the death.

- Coroner's clerks who provide information and assist the parents during the preparation for the inquest into the death of their child.

- Funeral directors and staff who assist the parents with the arrangements for their child's funeral.

- The media, the sudden death of a child will attract newspaper reporters.

At the beginning of this chapter it was stated that the professional carer's manner and attitude, towards the family members, could have a significant effect on the individual, and can influence how the person will cope following the death. It is therefore, desirable that those carers are motivated to provide comfort and support, in addition to the necessary practical care. It was indicated by Wertheimer that the care provided to the family by embarrassed and inexperienced staff, compared unfavourably with the supportive and compassionate care provided by experienced staff [1].

Information should be provided in writing, for the parents, on local and national agencies that are able to provide on-going support should this be required; they are unlikely to retain information given verbally when experiencing emotional turmoil.

The local minister can be of great assistance to the parents and family when they are endeavouring to decide on the form that the service should take, as the funeral may help to provide great comfort and a lasting happy memory. However, the family gathering may provide a forum for recriminations, especially if the parents were separated, or divorced, at the time of the young person's suicide [3].

ON-GOING CARE AND SUPPORT

Suicide of a young person has been described as a triple burden, by one parent; firstly there is the sudden death, secondly the death of their child, and thirdly the stigma of suicide [1]. It is therefore not surprising that once the activity of completing the practical processes is over the intense emotions experienced by the parents, at the time of the child's death, may return as the finality of the act registers. The parent may feel overwhelmed by guilt and be convinced that he or she has been a bad parent [6]; and may also wonder what he or she had done to have such an unhappy child. Brothers and sisters may feel that it was their fault, especially if they had recently had an argument with the young person[7].

During the early period of mourning the parents, who may be consumed by their own grief, may not notice how unhappy the brothers and sisters are during this time[8].

The attitude of neighbours who may imply blame can contribute to the parent's feeling of guilt, and in addition any hostility from relatives can intensify those feelings.

At the time of the inquest press reporters may add to the distress of the family if the reporting is sensational. Bolton found that a pro-active attempt to minimise sensational press reporting helped, and that it was beneficial to allow a friend or relative to prepare a story for the press[2].

The head teacher or college principal will need to be informed of the young person's death by the parents. This is when it could be useful to use the Local Action Plan (as described in the following chapter), in an attempt to provide support to staff and pupils when they hear the tragic news of their young friend's death. Teaching staff should anticipate that the death may have an adverse effect on the school performance of brothers and sisters of the young person.

Opinions appear to be in agreement that the on-going use of medication, or alcohol should be avoided by the parents[1, 3, 9]; although, it is acknowledged that the use of medication, during the first few days following their child's death, could be helpful. However, at some stage the bereavement will have to be experienced without medication and alcohol to dull the pain. Should the grief reaction become overwhelming and not abate, then it could become necessary for the parent, brother or sister to receive professional help. Although a relevant organisation may be able to provide this help during the crisis, the quantity and quality of on-going care will depend on local availability[6].

Each family member will have their own unique way of grieving, and this may lead to difficulties and resentment if this is not understood by the family. The father may find it difficult to express his emotions, and will also be expected to return to work a short time after the death of his child. His suffering will be no less that that of the mother who may outwardly express her grief as she remains at home surrounded by the memories of her child [8]. The family may become more united in their grief, or alternatively the suicide may lead to the break-up of the family; although, Wrobleski indicated that the underlying cause for marital disharmony was likely to have been present before the suicide [3].

Grandparents can also be deeply affected by the tragedy as, in addition to their own grief, they will also have to see their own child grieving over the loss of their grandchild [10].

The reaction of professional carers and friends towards the family during the grieving period, which could be acute and last for many months or years, can either help or hinder the individual family member throughout this time.

In this chapter the impact of that single act, the suicide of a child, and its effect on the parents, other family members and the young person's local community network has been examined. Although life can never be the same again for the parents and family, Wrobleski urges that life has to go on and it may help to remember 'that the worst that can happen already has' [3]. It has also been observed by Wright that parents and families experience overwhelming disasters and yet still have the strength and ability to move forward [11].

This chapter is concluded with a phrase that is used by Kubler-Ross during her work with bereaved parents :

'Out of every tragedy can come a blessing or a curse - compassion or bitterness - the choice is yours' [9].

SECTION THREE

PREVENTION AND QUALITY CARE

6. PREVENTIVE CARE

Evidence provided from the studies explored in the first four chapters of this book indicates that not enough has been done to raise awareness of the need for suicide prevention work among young people worldwide. The devastating effect, following the suicide of a child, on a high number of people that included teachers and school friends in addition to family members was explored in the previous chapter.

It was implied that suicide prophylaxis should begin at birth, and progress throughout life, through the creation of psychological conditions which aim to prevent the occurrence of suicide [1, 2]. It has also been recognised that society should invest the same amount of energy in promoting a child's emotional and mental well-being, as that invested in physical well-being [3]. Although this is a situation to strive for there is little evidence available that action to achieve this is taking place at present. It would, therefore, appear necessary to look at preventive action that should be taken now in an attempt to reduce the rate of suicide and attempted suicide of young people.

EMOTIONAL HEALTH

The roots of suicidal behaviour lie in many different social, health and educational problems experienced by young people, and it has been recommended that suicide prevention should include the self-destructive behaviours of :

-    substance abuse, and

-    eating disorders [4].

Teachers, ministers, health and social workers work in a situation where they could influence and assist parents in the adoption of methods to promote good psychological and mental health of the child.

Crook identified the parent as the most important person in the life of the teenagers who took part in a study on attempted suicide [5]. Other findings in the study included :

-    the importance of listening to the teenager, instead of lecturing;

- the need to help the teenager deal with stress and emotional pain;
- the need to increase the teenager's self-esteem through praise and encouragement;
- the need to enable the teenager to become independent, while at the same time staying involved and supportive.

Other investigators recommended that parents and carers should take time from their busy schedule to praise and boost the self-esteem of the child [6, 7].

The reality of the present high rate of unemployment among young people, internationally, and its effect on self-esteem has been acknowledged [7, 8]. Help will need to be given to these young people to enable them to :

- explore and find new ways of living a meaningful life in the absence of work; and
- find ways of investing themselves, without a loss of self-worth, towards a future that may be different from their expectations of a life of full-time work [8, 9].

Friends and peers have an important role to play in helping to identify vulnerable young people. It has been found that at the time of attempted suicide, and suicide, some children and adolescents had undiagnosed depression and may have benefitted from medical care had this been diagnosed earlier [10, 11].

The use of a health diary or journal by the child has received encouragement from some health carers and teachers; this acts as a means for the young person to record his, or her, feelings if unable to discuss the emotions felt. However, Progoff advised carers to be aware that diaries and journals could be used in a judgmental way against the self [12].

Inevitably, life can be painful and one of the challenges of life is learning to cope with emotional and physical pain; although there could be times when young people need help in order to tolerate failure and learn to develop their inner resources [9].

A study that identified how 8 - 12 year olds coped with stressful events in their lives categorised the actions taken by the children into the following groups :

- relaxation
- physical exercise
- spiritual
- verbal aggression
- isolation, and
- physical aggression

The researcher indicated that the 8 - 9 year old child experimented with a greater variety of coping strategies than the older children who preferred to use the action that worked best for them [13].

It would be helpful to discuss emotional and mental health concepts more openly with young people in a supportive environment, such as the home, classroom and school clinic. This could assist towards removing the stigma that still appears to be attached to mental health issues. The importance of recognising the early signs of sadness and despair, that could indicate an underlying depression, has been emphasised in many studies [5, 10, 11, 14].

LOCAL ACTION PLAN

It has been indicated that a local action plan should be available in anticipation that a young person, who is living in the locality, may commit suicide [4]. The plan could then be brought into use, if needed at any time, in a similar way that a major incident plan is available in case of a major incident in the locality. The local action plan could provide assistance to carers and :

- prevent a feeling of panic should the tragedy of suicide of a child take place, and
- facilitate an effective response to the needs of other children in the locality who could be confused and upset at the death of a friend.

The carers who need to be consulted when drawing up a local action plan include :

- Director of Public Health

- Teachers

- School Nurse

- Minister of Religion

- Psychologist

- Police

- Child Psychiatrist

- Probation Officer

- Social Worker

- General Practitioner, and

- Voluntary Sector representatives of the relevant local agencies.

One advantage of having a local plan is to lessen the risk of so-called 'experts' descending on the community when the suicide takes place [4]. Wrobleski advised against listening to 'experts' who state that young people should not attend the funeral of their friend, and should not be encouraged to grieve openly when a child dies following the act of suicide [15].

PRIMARY, SECONDARY AND TERTIARY PREVENTION

In the following paragraphs the use of the terms primary, secondary and tertiary preventive action will be discussed.

Primary Prevention refers to the work of different agencies that may respond to a request for help from a young person who is distressed and desolate.

Childline is a agency that was set up to deal specifically with all types of problems of children and adolescents who live in England. However the limited number of available telephone 'helplines' to deal with the calls from young people could indicate that the child may be unable to make contact with the helper at the 'helpline' on occasions.

The Samaritans Organisation has links throughout the world and responds to the needs of suicidal people of all age groups. The success rate in prevention of suicide of young, white females has been acknowledged, although reservations on effectiveness with other groups of people have been expressed

[15, 16]. It has been suggested that a more accurate term to describe primary prevention is 'intervention at the time of the crisis' [15].

Other primary prevention agencies include the 'Walk in' clinics that are to be found in cities and towns. The availability of these clinics will depend on the local resources to fund these initiatives [17].

Secondary Prevention involves the care of a young person following a suicide attempt and includes the care of the family. On-going support and care of the young person and family is advised as a means of enabling any future problems to be dealt with in a supportive environment. Attendance at the follow-up clinic does not always take place and this may be influenced by either carer or parental attitude.

Tertiary Prevention refers to the care of the family and others who are psychologically close to the young person who died following a suicide act, this may include teachers and school friends.

ROLE OF SOCIETY

Studies on suicide prevention appear inconclusive with regard to the effectiveness of different interventions [4, 10]. There would appear to be agreement that :

- local small-scale multidisciplinary intervention programmes should be undertaken, prior to large-scale intervention work on suicide prevention among young people.

It was also agreed that there is a need for :

- early detection of symptoms of depression, and

- local programmes to include work on the other self-destructive behaviours of substance abuse and eating disorders.

It has been recommended that the public should be given access to information and education from health carers regarding current knowledge on prevention, signs and symptoms and treatment of suicidal behaviour [4]. Although a major problem that remains to be tackled was identified by Stengel who raised the question of how contact could be established between lonely young people in despair and those people who want to help them [2].

It is unlikely that there will be sufficient professional carers to cope with the rising rate of suicidal behaviour of young people, therefore it is likely to be necessary for the foreseeable future for society to unite in an endeavour to reverse the trend. It is inevitable that prevention will have to become a part of everybody's daily life if society is to make progress in the reduction of the tragic loss of young life.

This chapter is concluded with a statement from 'Young Minds' :

'Young Minds knows that the cost of neglecting children's mental health is very high, needless suffering, waste of potential, and more complex long term problems. And we cannot forget that our children are the adults and parents of tomorrow' [18].

7.   QUALITY CARE -
CONCLUSIONS AND RECOMMENDATIONS

CONCLUSIONS

The conclusions reached following the study of suicidal children and adolescents are stated in the following paragraphs. Recommendations are made at the end of the chapter.

RECORD KEEPING

The suicidal deaths recorded are lower than the suspected number of deaths and evidence on the cause of death may be inconclusive unless a suicide note is available. There would not appear to be either national or international systems in operation for the routine collection of statistics on attempted suicide in young people. Local record systems appear to be the exception rather than the rule and there is no systematic co-ordination of statistics from local hospital and local doctors' community based premises. The difficulty in obtaining accurate statistics on suicidal behaviour could be linked to either the cultural aspect or the negative attitudes that still prevail towards a suicidal act.

THE CHILD'S RIGHTS

The rights of the child have received more publicity during the past decade, although much more work remains to be done to enable the child's lone voice to be heard especially when in the presence of professional carers.

COMPLEXITY OF SUICIDE

The possibility that undiagnosed depression could be an underlying cause of the child's suicidal behaviour is stated in many of the studies. However the theories of Stengel and Durkheim on impulsivity, risk taking and the gamble with life appear relevant when studying suicidal behaviour today [1, 2]. The weak predictive power of suicide risk factors is of concern as it is not possible to identify which child will attempt suicide, or die following a suicidal act. It is known that a young person is especially vulnerable following a suicide attempt and that he or she may repeat the attempt, with a possible fatal outcome, during the following twelve month period [3].

PROVISION OF CARE

A suicide attempt is a meaningful and momentous event in the life of a young person, and the attitude of the professional carer can influence whether psychological and mental health care is accepted or rejected following the suicide attempt. The use of excessive restraint on the distressed child is unacceptable practice and a written policy on restraint of young people is required in an organisation's department(s).

In some departments a suicidal child is kept waiting for a lengthy period before :

- admission to an appropriate hospital ward, and

- assessment by a member of the mental health care team.

This is unsafe and unacceptable care.

The problem of non-attendance of the child and family at the follow-up clinic appointment is of concern and requires action to find a solution to the problem. The missed appointments could mean that the valuable and scarce resource of professional skills and time is wasted.

The personal act of a child's suicide has profound social implications. Professional carers face a great challenge and responsibility as they endeavour to minimise the emotional trauma, shock and grief experienced by the parents and family following the suicide. It is known that a carer can adversely affect the parent's recovery from grief should an unintentional careless or thoughtless remark be made following the death of the child [4].

The provision of written information for the young person who attempts suicide, and also for the parents following their child's suicide is essential. The names and addresses of voluntary organisations that are able to provide help and support to the child, parents and family should be included, along with the practical details and information, as this may be required following the crisis or at a later period.

SUICIDE PREVENTION

The task of reducing the rates of suicide and attempted suicide in young people by planned action will not be easy and presents a challenge to society. Thirty years ago Stengel stated that suicide prophylaxis should begin at birth, and before, in order to bring about a reduction in suicidal acts[2]. Regrettably some of the factors that have an adverse effect on suicide risk appear to be on the increase, internationally, and include :

- substance abuse

- unemployment rate

- lack of a stable family life.

It is therefore essential that the child should be a target worldwide for suicide intervention and prevention work. It is unfortunate that the child, and especially the male child, is reluctant to seek help for psychological and mental health problems. At present there would not appear to be a ready cure for suicidal behaviour and efforts will need to be directed where some impact can be made. Because the impulse factor is difficult to identify in a child it is agreed by many health carers that efforts should be concentrated on the early detection of depressive illness in young people. However, the use of local small-scale research programmes into suicide prevention that include all types of suicidal behaviour could be beneficial.

Teachers have a vital role to play in the early detection of depression through observation of changes in the child's performance and behaviour at school; especially when a parent does not notice or does not accept that the child may have a problem. Referral of the child for health care advice is recommended when psychological and mental health problems are suspected by parents and teachers. The message that it is acceptable practice for a child to seek psychological and mental health care from his or her local doctor, in addition to physical care, should be reinforced periodically by parents and professional carers.

LOCAL ACTION PLAN

A community may find it helpful to have a local action plan available in the event of the death of a child following a suicidal act. This local action plan could be used, with slight modification, in the event of the sudden death of a child(ren) from other causes for example - murder or motor vehicle accident.

Finally it is necessary to find ways within the local community of establishing contact between young people who are desolate, lonely and depressed and those carers who want to provide help. Only then will the rising rate in destruction and waste of young life stand a chance of being reversed.

RECOMMENDATIONS

RECORD KEEPING

1(a)   A system should be available to maintain accurate records within a local area on

- attempted suicide of young people

- suicide of young people.

(b)   The hospital and community statistics on suicide and attempted suicide of young people should be co-ordinated at the local area.

(c)   Records at the local area level should be sub-divided into age and gender bands in accordance with the system adopted by the World Health Organisation e.g., 5 - 14, 15 - 24 years. Additional subdivisions should be introduced as necessary e.g., 10 - 14

2   Local standards should be agreed and introduced on acceptable waiting periods for :

- provision of care in the accident and emergency department

- transfer to an appropriate ward/department from the accident and emergency department.

- assessment by a member of the child and adolescent mental health care team.

The standard should be monitored and remedial action taken as required.

3   A record should be kept on non-attendance at follow-up clinic appointments. A system should be in place to ascertain the reason for non-attendance at the clinic, e.g. inconvenient appointment time, cost of travel etc.

CHILDREN AND THEIR RIGHTS

Professional carers should be aware of the contents of the UN Convention on the Rights of the Child which includes the following articles :

Rights to Life - Children have a right to life and to the best possible chance to develop fully.

Access to Information - Children should be able to get hold of a wide range of information, especially any which would make life better for them.

Day to Day Care - Any child being looked after away from home in a boarding school, long stay institution or hospital must also receive proper care.

PROVISION OF CARE

1 Open discussion on the following ethical issues should be encouraged among carers in a supportive environment :

- rights of the child

- the meaning of life

- the value of life.

An experienced professional carer should be available to facilitate discussion and debate on the issues.

2 Sensitive non-judgmental care should be available for the child and parent from an experienced professional carer :

- before the onset of the crisis

- at the time of the crisis

- following the crisis.

3 Information in writing should be given to the child or parent on :

- local voluntary services that are available

- local statutory services that are available and the nature of the service, e.g., financial support, the work of the coroner, walk-in clinics.

4 Use of Control

An agreed policy on the use of control should be available, in writing, in all departments. The policy should be reviewed and updated periodically.

SUICIDE PREVENTION

1   Professional carers and parents should incorporate psychological, mental and physical health as a single topic of discussion with the child from an early age.

2   Professional carers and parents should enable the child to express his or her feelings without fear of ridicule. This need is especially great for the male child who is reluctant to seek help with psychological and mental health problems.

3   Small-scale local research studies should be undertaken on :

-    early detection of depressive illness in childhood

-    suicidal behaviour in young people including substance abuse and eating disorders

-    'Drop in' advice centre on psychological, mental and physical health.

4   A local Action Plan should be available in the event of the death of a child through suicide and other incidents of sudden death.

5   A professional health carer should be responsible for the provision, periodically, of an education programme on developments in suicide prevention work for carers, parents and members of the local community.

6   Innovative work should be undertaken by professional carers in an endeavour to establish contact between the sad, lonely, desolate and depressed child and the carer.

REFERENCES

GLOSSARY

1   Hoghughi, M. Assessing Child and Adolescent Disorders, *London*, Sage Publications Ltd., 1992.

2   Stengel, E. Suicide and Attempted Suicide, *England*, MacGibbon and Key Ltd., 1964.

INTRODUCTION

1   World Health Organization. World Health Statistics Annual - 1992, *Geneva*, 1993.

2   Stengel, E. Suicide and Attempted Suicide, *England*, MacGibbon and Kee Ltd., 1964.

3   Durkheim, E. Suicide, (translated by Spaulding J and Simpson G), *London*, Routledge & Kegan Paul Ltd., 1952.

4   Brooksbank, D. Suicide and Parasuicide in Childhood and Early Adolescence, British Journal of Psychiatry, 1985, 146 pp 459-463.

5   Fahy, T. Suicide and the Irish : From Sin to Serotonin, In : Keane, C (Editor), Mental Health in *Ireland*, Dublin, Gill and McMillan, 1991.

6   Wrobleski, A. Suicide : Why? *United States of America*, Afterwords Publishing, 1989.

7   Department of Health. The Children Act and Local Authorities : A Guide for Parents, *United Kingdom*, September 1991.

8   Department of Health. The Rights of the Child - A Guide to the UN Convention, *England*, 1993.

9   Bryan, J. Depression, *London*, Channel 4 Television, 1994.

CHAPTER 1

1   World Health Organisation. World Health Statistics Annual - 1992, *Geneva*, 1993.

2   Durkheim, E. Suicide, (translated by Spaulding, J and Simpson, G), *London*, Routledge & Kegan Paul Ltd., 1952.

3   Stengel, E. Suicide and Attempted Suicide, *England*, MacGibbon and Kee Ltd., 1964.

4   Fahy, T. Suicide and the Irish : From Sin to Serotonin, In : Keane, C, (Editor), Mental Health in Ireland, *Dublin*, Gill and McMillan, 1991.

5   Brooksbank, D. Suicide and Parasuicide in Childhood and early Adolescence, British Journal of Psychiatry, 1985, 146, 459-463.

6   Crook, M. Please, Listen to Me ! *Canada*, International Self-Counsel Press Ltd., (2nd edition) 1992.

7   Curran, D. Adolescent Suicidal Behaviour, *United States of America*, Hemisphere Publishing Corporation, 1987.

8   Mann, J, Demeo, M, Keilp, J and McBride, P. Biological Correlates of Suicidal Behaviour, in Pfeffer, C (Editor) Suicide among Youth, *United States of America*, American Psychiatric Press Inc., 1989.

9   Wrobleski, A. Suicide : Survivors, *United States of America*, Afterwords Publishing, 1991.

10   Wertheimer, A. A Special Scar, *London*, Routledge, 1991.

11   Bolton, I. My Son – My Son, *United States of America*, Bolton Press, (7th edition) 1987.

12   Eldrid, J. Caring for the Suicidal, *London*, Constable, 1988.

13   Lake, T. Living with Grief, *United Kingdom*, Sheldon Press, SPCK, 1984.

14   Harris, J. The Value of Life, *London*, Routledge & Kegan Paul Plc, 1985.

15   Brown J, Kitson, A and McKnight, T. Challenges in Caring, *London*, Chapman and Hall, 1992.

16   The Samaritans. School Project, *United Kingdom*, 1993.

17   Department of Health (DOH). Permissible Forms of Control in Children's Residential Care, *London*, DOH, 1993.

18   Royal College of Psychiatrists. The Management of Parasuicide in Young People under Sixteen, *London*, Bulletin, 1982, pp182-185.

19   Fogarty, M. A Difficult Age, London, Nursing Times, August 4th, 1993, Volume 89, No 31, pp 18-19.

20   NHS Advisory Service. Bridges Over Troubled Waters, *England*, HMSO, 1986.

21   Townsend, P and Davidson, N (editors). Inequalities in Health : The Black Report, *England*, Penguin Books, 1992.

22   Whitehead, M. The Health Divide, in Townsend, P and Davidson, N (editors) Inequalities in Health, *England*, Penguin Books, 1992.

23   Kumar, V. Poverty and Inequality in the UK - The Effects on Children, *London*, National Children's Bureau, 1993.

24   Hewlett, S. Child Neglect in Rich Nations, *United States of America*, United Nations Children's Fund, 1993.

25   Klerman, G. The Current Age of Youthful Melancholia, *England*, British Journal of Psychiatry, 1988, 152 pp 4-14.

26 Bradshaw, J. Home Coming, *United States of America*, Piatkus, 1990.

27 Fahy, T. Suicide and the Irish : From Sin to Serotonin, in : Keane, C, (editor), Mental Health in Ireland, *Dublin*, Gill and McMillan, 1991.

28 Bryan, J. Depression, *London*, Channel 4 Television, 1994.

29 Bowlby, J. The Making and Breaking of Affectional Bonds, *London*, Tavistock/Routledge Publication, 1979.

30 Jewett, C. Helping Children Cope with Separation and Loss, *London*, B T Batsford Ltd., 1984.

31 Turner, T. Balancing Act for Families, *London*, Nursing Times, April 13 1994, Volume 90, No 15, pp 16-17.

32 Siegart, M. How we Betray Children, *London*, The Times, April 11 1994, p 14.

CHAPTER 2

1 Fahy, T. Suicide And The Irish : From Sin To Serotonin In : Keane, C (Editor), Mental Health In Ireland, *Dublin*, Gill And Mcmillan, 1991.

2 Wrobleski, A. Suicide Why? *Minneapolis*, Afterwords Publishing, 1989.

3 Stengel, E. Suicide And Attempted Suicide, *England*, Macgibbon And Kee Ltd., 1964.

4 Mann, J, Demeo, M, Keilp, J And Mcbride, P. Biological Correlates Of Suicidal Behaviour In Youth In : Pfeffer, C (Editor), Suicide Among Youth, *United States Of America*, American Psychiatric Press Inc., 1989.

5 Roy, A. Genetics And Suicidal Behaviour In : Pfeffer, C (Editor), Suicide Among Youth, *United States Of America*, American Psychiatric Press Inc., 1989.

6 Brooksbank, D. Suicide And Parasuicide In Childhood And Early Adolescence, *England*, British Journal Of Psychiatry, 1985, 146 Pp 459-463.

7 Bryan, J. Depression, *London*, Channel 4 Television, 1994.

8 Durkheim, E. Suicide (Translated By Spaulding, J And Simpson, G), *London*, Routledge & Kegan Paul Ltd., 1952.

9 Klerman, G. The Current Age Of Melancholia, *England*, British Journal Of Psychiatry, 1988, 152, Pp 4-14.

10 Crook, M. Please, Listen To Me!, *Canada*, International Self-Counsel Press Ltd., (2nd Edition) 1992.

11 Fitzgerald, M. The Child And The Family In : Keane, C (Editor), Mental Health In Ireland, *Dublin*, Gill And Mcmillan, 1991.

12 Pearce, J. Fighting, Teasing And Bullying, *England*, Thorsons Publishers Ltd., 1989.

13 Eldrid, J. Caring For The Suicidal, *London*, Constable, 1988.

14 Hoberman, H And Garfinkel, B. Completed Suicide In Youth In : Pfeffer, C (Editor), Suicide Among Youth, *United States Of America*, American Psychiatric Press Inc., 1989.

15 Pierce, A. Suicide Of A Bullied Schoolgirl, *London*, The Times, 15 April 1994.

16 Wertheimer, A. A Special Scar, *London*, Routledge, 1991.

CHAPTER 3

1 Stengel, E. Suicide and Attempted Suicide, *England*, MacGibbon and Kee Ltd., 1964.

2 The Royal College of Psychiatrists, The Management of Parasuicide in Young People under Sixteen, *England*, Bulletin, October 1982, pp 182-185.

3 Brooksbank, D. Suicide and Parasuicide in Childhood and Early Adolescence, *England*, British Journal of Psychiatry, 1985, 146, pp 459-463.

4 Crook, M. Please, Listen to Me! *Canada*, International Self-Counsel Press Ltd., (2nd edition), 1992.

5 Lawler, J. Behind the Screens, *Edinburgh*, Churchill Livingstone 1991.

6 Wright, B. Caring in Crisis, *Edinburgh*, Churchill Livingstone (2nd edition) 1993.

7 Eldrid, J. Caring for the Suicidal, *London*, Constable, 1988.

8 NHS Advisory Service. Bridges Over Troubled Waters, *England*, HMSO, 1986.

9 McKeon, P. Depression in Ireland in : Keane, C (editor), Mental Health in Ireland, *Dublin*, Gill and McMillan, 1991.

CHAPTER 4

1 Wright, B. Caring in Crisis, *Edinburgh*, Churchill Livingstone, (2nd edition), 1993.

2 NHS Advisory Service. Bridges Over Troubled Waters, *England*, HMSO, 1986.

3 Stengel, E. Suicide and Attempted Suicide, *England*, MacGibbon and Kee Ltd., 1964.

4 Crook, M. Every Parent's Guide to Understanding Teenagers and Suicide, *Canada*, International Self-Counsel Press Ltd., 1988.

5 Brooksbank, D. Suicide and Parasuicide in Childhood and Early Adolescence, *England*, British Journal of Psychiatry, 1985, 146 pp 459-463.

6   Child Psychotherapy Trust. Newsletter, *England*, Winter 1993.

7   Lake, T. Living with Grief, *United Kingdom*, Sheldon Press SPCK, 1984.

8   Lendrum, S and Syme, G. Gift of Tears, *London*, Routledge, 1992.

CHAPTER 5

1   Wertheimer, A. A Special Scar, London, Routledge, 1991.

2   Bolton, I. My Son – My Son, *United States of America*, Bolton Press, (7th edition), 1987.

3   Wrobleski, A. Suicide : Survivors, *United States of America*, Afterwords Publishing, 1991.

4   Stengel, E. Suicide and Attempted Suicide, *England*, MacGibbon and Kee Ltd., 1964.

5   The Compassionate Friends. Preparing for your Child's Funeral, *England*, 1993.

6   Crook, M. Please, Listen to Me! *Canada*, International Self-Counsel Press Ltd., (2nd edition), 1992.

7   The Compassionate Friends. Helping Younger Bereaved Brothers and Sisters, *England*, 1993.

8   The Compassionate Friends. Grieving Couples, *England*, 1993.

9   Kubler-Ross, E. On Children and Death, *New York*, MacMillan Publishing Co., 1983.

10 The Compassionate Friends. To Bereaved Grandparents, *England*, 1993.

11 Wright, B. Caring in Crisis, *Edinburgh*, Churchill Livingstone, (2nd edition) 1993.

CHAPTER 6

1   Fahy, T. Suicide and the Irish : From Sin to Serotonin in : Keane, C. (editor), Mental Health in Ireland, *Dublin*, Gill and McMillan, 1991.

2   Stengel, E. Suicide and Attempted Suicide, *England*, MacGibbon and Kee Ltd., 1964.

3   Frazier, S. Foreword in : Pfeffer, C (editor) Suicide Among Youth, *United States of America*, American Psychiatric Press Inc., 1989.

4   Rosenberg, M, Eddy, D, Wolpert, R and Broumas, E. Developing Strategies to Prevent Youth Suicide in : Pfeffer, C (editor) Suicide Among Youth, *United States of America*, American Psychiatric Press Inc., 1989.

5   Crook, M. Please, Listen to Me! *Canada*, International Self-Counsel Press Ltd., (2nd edition) 1992.

6   Bolton, I. My Son – My Son, *United States of America*, Bolton Press (7th edition), 1987.

7   Hewlett, S. Child Neglect in Rich Nations, *United States of America*, United Nations Children's Fund, 1993.

8 Watkins, S. Unemployment and Health in : World Health, *Geneva*, World Health Organization, November-December 1992, pp 18-19.

9 Eldrid, J. Caring for the Suicidal, *London*, Constable, 1988.

10 Brooksbank, D. Suicide and Parasuicide in Childhood and Early Adolescence, *England*, British Journal of Psychiatry, 1985, 146, pp 459-463.

11 Bryan, J. Depression, *London*, Channel 4 Television, 1994.

12 Progoff, I. At a Journal Workshop, *United States of America*, Dialogue House Library, 1975.

13 Ryan-Wenger, N. Development and Psychometric Properties of the Schoolagers' Coping Strategies Inventory in : Nursing Research, *United States of America*, AJN Company, November-December 1990, Vol 39, No 6 pp 344-349

14 Klerman, G. The Current Age of Youthful Melancholia, *England*. British Journal of Psychiatry, 1988, 152 pp 4-14.

15 Wrobleski, A. Suicide : Survivors, *United States of America*, Afterwords Publishing, 1991.

16 Hollinger, P. Epidemiologic Issues in Youth Suicide in : Pfeffer, C (editor) Suicide Among Youth, *United States of America*, American Psychiatric Press Inc., 1989.

17 Armstrong, E. Mental Health Check, *London*, Nursing Times, August 18 Vol 89, No 33, 1993, pp 40-41.

18 Young Minds. Growing Pains..... or Signs of Trouble? *London*, Young Minds Trust, 1994.

CHAPTER 7

1 Durkheim, E. Suicide (translated by Spaulding, J and Simpson, G.), *London*, Routledge & Kegan Paul Ltd., 1952.

2 Stengel, E. Suicide and Attempted Suicide, *England*, MacGibbon and Kee Ltd., 1964.

3 Brooksbank, D. Suicide and Parasuicide in Childhood and Early Adolescence, *England*, British Journal of Psychiatry, 1985, 146 pp 459-463.

4 Wertheimer, A. A Special Scar, *London*, Routledge, 1991

APPENDIX A

1 Kitson, A. Dynamic Standard Setting, *London*, Royal College of Nursing, 1990.

AUDIT TOOL

The publication of numerous Government charters, guidelines and efficiency tables would appear to indicate that standards of care are under scrutiny. The information contained in this appendix may be of assistance to carers who are endeavouring to audit activity in the workplace.

The audit 'tool kit' is intended to be used as a guide (e.g., i, ii, iii, iv). It is recommended that carers add relevant problem topics as necessary.

(i)   Outcome statement
(ii)   Outcome standard
(iii)   Measurement method
(iv)   Scoring system

Carers are advised to discuss audit activities with their local manager from the start, as it may become necessary to make changes in order to improve the quality of care.

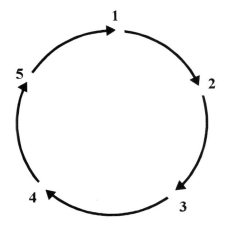

An Audit Cycle.

1. Problem identification

2. Outcome standard statement

3. Evaluate care

4. Decide on remedial action

5. Re-evaluation

(i)   OUTCOME STATEMENT

An outcome statement is a phrase or sentence that states the desired outcome.

TOPIC	OUTCOME STATEMENT	YES	NO	N/A	COMMENT
Rights of the Child	1. There is a copy of the United Nations Convention on the Rights of the Child in the department.				
Record Keeping	2. There is a system in operation in the department to record the number of children who : a. attempt suicide b. die following a suspected suicide act				
	3. There is an agreed standard in the department on the maximum length of time considered acceptable for a child to wait for : a. care following a suicide attempt b. assessment from a member of the mental health care team				
Inter-personal Care	4. The child is approached in a gentle and kind manner.				
	5. The child receives the carer's full attention.				
	6. The child is given an opportunity to explain his/her feelings.				
	7. The child receives sensitive and non-judgmental care that communicates worth and dignity.				
	8. An atmosphere of trust develops rather than one of power and authority.				
Communication	9. Written information is provided on care available from both statutory and voluntary agencies for : a. the child b. the parent				

Topic	Outcome Statement	Yes	No	N/A	Comment
Communication (Continued)	10. A written policy relating to permissible forms of control is available in the department (i.e., the use of physical restraint), and : a. after any incident, relating to the policy, a written report is made available immediately. b. carers and managers review each incident to ensure that any physical response does not exceed the agreed standard.				
	11. Effective procedures are in place, following a suicide/suicide attempt of a child, for confidential communication with : - health carer - clergy - teacher - social worker (as necessary)				
Suicide Prevention	12. Small-scale research studies on suicidal behaviour are undertaken in the local area.				
	13. The studies incorporate : a. substance abuse b. eating disorders				
	14. A nominated health carer is responsible for an education programme on developments in suicidal behaviour and care.				
	15. The education programme is provided for : a. professional carers b. parents and the local population				
	16. A Local Action Plan is available in anticipation of a child's suicide.				
	17. A local programme of action to enable contact to be made with the lonely, desolate and depressed child has been implemented.				

(ii)   OUTCOME STANDARD

An outcome standard is aimed at measuring the process of care and comparing the outcome with the stated standard.
Example :

Problem identified : Low attendance rate (less than 50%) at child and family mental health clinic.

Standard statement : A 90% attendance rate will be achieved at the child and family mental health clinic. (Standard agreed May 1994).

Evaluation date - September 1994
Achieve by date - December 1994

Structure	Process	Outcome
Skilled staff	Carers demonstrate sensitive/non-judgmental attitude.	Child and Parent attend clinic.
Appointment system	Suitable appointment time given.	
Financial assistance for child/parent	Information given on available funds.	
Supervised play area for young children	Children receive supervised play.	
Clinic venue	Transport available for distant venues.	

(Modified Kitson [1])

(iii)   MEASUREMENT METHODS

Observation - This method can be useful when it is more important to measure an event than an opinion.

Checklist - For use during a period of observation and during an interviw.

Interview - A useful method when personal opinion is important. The interview techniques require skilled personnel to conduct the following three different kinds of interview :

-    formal/structured
-    informal/semi-structured
-    open/unstructured.

Review of Care Record - A study of the written care record by an experienced professional carer. The record provides a retrospective impression of the care.

Questionnaire - This method requires careful planning prior to implementation. It can be useful for a survey of opinion from a high number of people.

Diary - A method which may be useful to encourage a child to record her/his feelings and thoughts about the standard of care.

(iv)   SCORING SYSTEM

Two examples are given of a scoring system in (a) and (b).

(a) Each outcome statement has a possible response of 'yes' or 'no' or 'not applicable' (N/A), a column is also included for comment.

Number of positive responses x 100   =   Audit Score

e.g.   Number of questions   =   12
        Number of N/A responses   =   2 (-2)
        Total applicable responses   =   10
        Number of 'yes' responses   =   6 (e.g., 6/10)

        Audit score   =   60%

(b) May be used to observe care being given.

	3	2	1	0	Comment
Outcome Statement	Best care	Average	Poor care	Unacceptable	
Agreed safety measures are carried out to prevent the child from self-harm.					

USEFUL ORGANISATIONS

FOR CHILDREN	
Child Line Royal Mail Building Studd Street LONDON N1 0QW Telephone : 071 239 1000 Child Line : 0800 1111	Free national helpline for children with any problem, in trouble or danger. 24 Hours a day, every day of the year.
The Child Psychotherapy Trust 21 Maresfield Gardens LONDON NW3 5SH Telephone : 071 433 3867	For children with emotional difficulties. The Child Psychotherapy Trust is a national charity dedicated to increasing the number of child psychotherapists available throughout the United Kingdom to treat emotionally damaged children, and their families.
The Children's Legal Centre 20 Crompton Terrace LONDON N1 2UN Telephone : 01 359 6251 Advice Service : 14.00-17.00 hours weekdays.	Provides free and confidential advice and information on aspects of law and policy affecting the child in England and Wales. It is open to young people, and to parents, professionals and other adults working with young people.
The Samaritans 10 The Grove SLOUGH SL1 1QP Local telephone numbers available throughout numerous countries.	Volunteers who befriend people who are feeling desperate, lonely or suicidal.
Young Minds 22A Boston Place LONDON NW1 6ER Telephone : 071 724 7262	Young Minds advocates early intervention and the provision of effective multi-professional services.

FOR BEREAVED PARENTS

Cruse Bereavement Care Local Branches available throughout England	Bereavement counselling and information
The Compassionate Friends 53 North Street BRISTOL BS3 1EN Telephone : 0272 539639	An international organisation of bereaved parents offering friendship and understanding to other bereaved parents.
The Work of the Coroner Free leaflet published by the Home Office, England.	Some questions answered on the inquest, the Coroner and issue of death certificate.

INDEX